Cover and Book Design by Brittany Bacinski
Follow Brittany on Instagram @brittanybacinski
Follow Amber on Instagram @mishkadawn

Photo Credit: Brittany Bacinski, Holden Photographs, Brittany Jo Kruger,
Canva, Wainwright Images and Neveux Studios

Published by All Good Juju, 2019

# Hippie Eats.

**HIGH-VIBE, GLUTEN-FREE, SOY-FREE,
REFINED-SUGAR-FREE & VEGAN FRIENDLY
FLAVORFUL DISHES**

by: Brittany Bacinski
& Amber Fokken

Health is
wealth.

# Healthy noms
# from 2 hippie moms.

We made this book for you. But first, we made it for our families. We wanted a place, a book if you will, to keep our favorite recipes.

When anyone is sick or looking for a healthier alternative to old classics, we still get texts asking, "Hey Britt, what's that vegan potato soup recipe?" or "Hey Amber, how can I eat more plant-based?"

Whatever it is, we've got the recipes our loved ones love in this very book. And that's pretty special.

All recipes are original health-forward family favorites. These are meals we eat regularly. We've learned over the years how to prepare healthy, plant-heavy meals-- without sacrificing flavor. We hope you love these meals as much as we do.

Enjoy!
Peace, love & plants,
Brittany & Amber

# Contents.

# You don't have to eat less, you have to eat right.

# BREAKFAST

# NOMS

# PUMPKIN OAT BREAKFAST MUFFINS

## INGREDIENTS

- 2 cups oat flour
- 1/2 cup old fashioned oats (save 2 tbsp for muffin tops)
- 1 cup pumpkin puree
- 1/4 cup maple syrup
- 1/4 cup avocado oil
- 2 tsp vanilla extract
- 1/2 tsp baking soda
- 2 tsp baking powder
- ½ tsp salt
- 2 1/2 tsp pumpkin spice
- 1 tsp apple cider vinegar
- 1/2 teaspoon vanilla extract
- 1 egg or 1 flax egg to make vegan
- pinch of salt

**PREP TIME: 10 MINUTES**
**COOK TIME: 25-30 MINUTES**
**TOTAL TIME: 40 MINUTES**

## DIRECTIONS

1. In a medium bowl, combine all dry ingredients.
2. Preheat oven to 350 degrees F.
3. Spray a cupcake/muffin pan with coconut oil spray or grease with coconut oil.
4. In a large bowl, combine all the wet and dry ingredients. Mix using a large spoon, but do NOT over mix.
5. Using an ice-cream scoop or spoon, scoop the batter into each cupcake holder. Sprinkle dried rolled oats on tops.
6. Bake for 25-30 minutes, or until toothpick comes clean.
7. Serve warm and enjoy!

# LEMON RASPBERRY CHIA DONUTS

## INGREDIENTS

- 1 1/2 cup GF all-purpose flour
- 1 tbsp fresh lemon juice
- zest from 1 lemon
- 1 tsp lemon extract
- 2 tbsp of chia seeds
- 1 1/2 cup unsweetened coconut milk yogurt
- 1 cup coconut sugar
- 1 tsbp lemon extract
- 2 tbsp maple syrup
- 1 tsp baking powder
- 1/2 cup fresh raspberries
- 2 eggs or 2 flax eggs to make vegan

## DIRECTIONS

1. Combine dry ingredients into a mixing bowl.

2. Preheat oven to 350 degrees F.

3. Place wet ingredients into mixing bowl and mix until batter is smooth. Mix in raspberries, gently.

4. Place batter into donut pan (I found mine online), filling each donut half way to prevent overflowing.

5. Bake for 10 minutes or until toothpick comes clean.

6. Allow donuts to cool before serving. Makes 12 donuts.

**PREP TIME: 10 MINUTES**
**COOK TIME: 10 MINUTES**
**TOTAL TIME: 20 MINUTES**

# SWEET N SALTY OATMEAL COOKIE GRANOLA

## INGREDIENTS

- 4 cups rolled GF oats
- 1/4 cup vegan butter flavored coconut oil
- 2 tsp ground cinnamon
- 1/4 cup avocado oil
- 2 tbsp vanilla extract
- 1 cup of raisins
- 1 cup of maple syrup
- 2 tbsp chia seeds
- 2 tbsp hemp seeds
- pink himalayan sea salt

## DIRECTIONS

1. Combine wet and dry ingredients into a large mixing bowl.
2. Preheat oven to 300 degrees.
3. Gently toss granola mix until coated evenly with oil and spices.
4. Place onto baking sheet, spreading evenly to remove clumps and bake evenly. If you prefer chunky granola, don't worry about spreading out the mix too thin.
5. Bake for 10 minutes, then mix ingredients with spatula to ensure an even bake, then bake again for another 10 minutes or until golden brown.
6. Remove baking sheet and allow granola mix to cool for up to 1 hour or so. The granola will be crunchier over the time it cools. Lightly dust pink salt over the granola as it's cooling.
7. Enjoy granola over yogurt, fruit, with milk as a homemade cereal or eat it plain!

**PREP TIME: 10 MINUTES**
**COOK TIME: 20 MINUTES**
**TOTAL TIME: 30 MINUTES**

# STRAWBERRY CAKE VEGAN DONUTS

## INGREDIENTS

- 1 1/2 cup GF all-purpose flour
- 1 cup coconut sugar
- 2 tsp strawberry extract
- 2 tbsp maple syrup
- 1 tsp baking powder
- 1/2 cup strawberry puree
- 1/4 cup avocado oil
- 1/4 cup plant milk
- 1 tsp apple cider vinegar
- handful of vegan chocolate chips
  optional but recommended

## DIRECTIONS

1. Combine dry ingredients into a mixing bowl.

2. Preheat oven to 350 degrees F.

3. Place wet ingredients into mixing bowl and mix until batter is smooth. Mix in strawberry puree, gently.

4. Place batter into donut pan (I found mine online), filling each donut 1/2 way to prevent overflowing.

5. Bake for 10 minutes or until toothpick comes clean.

5. Allow donuts to cool before serving. Makes 6-8.

**PREP TIME: 10 MINUTES**
**COOK TIME: 10 MINUTES**
**TOTAL TIME: 20 MINUTES**

# CLASSIC BANANA JUJU PANCAKES

## INGREDIENTS

- 2 cups oat flour
- 2 eggs
- 1/4 tsp baking powder
- 1 cup flax milk (or more depending on desired thickness)
- 2 bananas
- 1 tbsp vanilla extract
- 2-3 tbsp maple syrup to sweeten
- 1 cup of blueberries optional but recommended
- sprinkle of cinnamon
- 1 tbsp flax meal

## DIRECTIONS

1. Combine wet and dry ingredients into a mixing bowl.
2. Mix with hand mixer until batter is smooth and evenly mixed. Let the batter sit for a minute or two. It will allow the baking powder to activate and make your pancakes extra fluffy.
3. Pour pancake batter onto well greased griddle.
4. Cook until golden on each sides, approximately one minute on each side. Makes approximately 6-8 pancakes.

**PREP TIME: 10 MINUTES**
**COOK TIME: 15 MINUTES**
**TOTAL TIME: 25 MINUTES**

# VEGAN BANANA JUJU PANCAKES

## INGREDIENTS

- 1 1/2 ripe bananas
- 2-3 tbsp maple syrup to sweeten
- 1 cup plant milk (more or less depending on desired thickness)
- 1 tsp vanilla extract
- 1 tsp baking power
- 1/4 tsp baking soda
- 2 cups GF all purpose flour
- sprinkle of cinnamon
- 1 tbsp flax meal
- 2 tbsp of avocado oil or soy-free melted vegan butter

## DIRECTIONS

1. Combine wet and dry ingredients into a mixing bowl.
2. Mix with hand mixer until batter is smooth and evenly mixed. Let the batter sit for a minute or two. It will allow the baking powder to activate and make your pancakes extra fluffy.
3. Pour pancake batter onto well greased griddle.
4. Cook until golden on each sides, approximately one minute on each side. Makes approximately 6-8 pancakes.

**PREP TIME: 10 MINUTES**
**COOK TIME: 15 MINUTES**
**TOTAL TIME: 25 MINUTES**

# BANANA BREAD BREAKFAST BARS

## INGREDIENTS

- 2 smashed bananas
- 2/3 cup almond butter
- 1 cup plant milk
- 1 cup oat flour
- 1/2 cup rolled oats
- 2 tsp vanilla extract
- 1 tsp baking powder
- 1/4 cup vegan chocolate chips
- 1 tbsp flax seed
- 1 tbsp avocado oil
- 1/4 tsp sea salt
- 1/2 tsp cinnamon

## DIRECTIONS

1. Preheat oven to 350 degrees and grease a 9x9 baking dish with oil.
2. In a large mixing bowl, mix together all ingredients, saving some chocolate chips for on top. Stir until evenly mixed.
3. Place dish in oven. Bake for 25 minutes.
4. Let cool for 10-15 minutes. Slice into bars and enjoy!

**PREP TIME: 5 MINUTES**
**COOK TIME: 25 MINUTES**
**TOTAL TIME: 30 MINUTES**

# WESTERN BRONCO HASHBROWNS

## INGREDIENTS

- 1/2 medium white onion, peeled and diced
- 3 cloves garlic, minced
- 1 green bell pepper, cored and diced
- 10 small yellow gold potatoes
- salt and pepper to taste
- avocado oil

## DIRECTIONS

1. Bring a large pot of water to a boil. Add quartered potatoes and simmer for 10-15 minutes, until potatoes are still firm, but can be pierced with a fork. Drain potatoes and cool slightly.
2. When potatoes are cool enough to handle, dice them into small cubes.
3. Add potatoes and ingredients and 1 tablespoon of avocado oil to a pan.
4. Cook, stirring often, until potatoes are golden brown and cooked through, about 15 minutes. Add more avocado oil as needed, and more salt and pepper to taste, Serve and enjoy!

**PREP TIME: 15 MINUTES**
**COOK TIME: 25 MINUTES**
**TOTAL TIME: 40 MINUTES**

# ICE-BOX BREAKFAST COOKIES

## INGREDIENTS

- 1 cup of GF rolled oats
- 4 tbsp of almond or cashew butter
- 1/4 cup raisins.
- 2 tbsp hemp seeds
- 1 tbsp chia seeds
- 1 tbsp ground flax seed
- 2 tbsp of honey
- 4 tbsp of melted vegan butter flavor coconut oil
- pinch of sea salt
- vegan chocolate chips (optional but recommeneded)

## DIRECTIONS

1. Combine all ingredients into one mixing bowl.
2. Roll into even balls on parchment paper (Makes about 4-6 small cookies)
3. Place in storage container and freeze for 1-3 hours.
4. Enjoy frozen for the best treat, they get melty rather quick!

**PREP TIME: 10 MINUTES**
**COOK TIME: 1-3 HOURS**
**TOTAL TIME: 1-3 HOURS**

# VEGGIE HEAVY CHICKPEA SCRAMBLE

## INGREDIENTS

- 1 can of chickpeas, drained and rinsed
- 2 cups broccoli
- 1/2 onion diced finely
- 1 1/2 tsp garlic powder
- 1 1/2 tsp onion powder
- 4 cups quartered potatoes
- 1 red bell pepper
- 1 cup yellow squash
- 1 cup zucchini
- 1 cup cherry tomatoes
- 1 tbsp avocado oil

## DIRECTIONS

1. Bring a large pot of water to a boil. Add quartered potatoes and simmer for 10-15 minutes, until potatoes are still firm, but can be pierced with a fork. Drain potatoes and cool slightly.
2. When potatoes are cool enough to handle, dice them into small cubes. Add potatoes, chickpeas and ingredients and 1 tablespoon of avocado oil to a pan.
3. Cook, stirring often, until potatoes are golden brown and cooked through, about 15 minutes. Add more avocado oil as needed, and more salt and pepper to taste,
4. Serve and enjoy!

**PREP TIME: 10 MINUTES**
**COOK TIME: 25 MINUTES**
**TOTAL TIME: 35 MINUTES**

# THE FAMOUS BREAKFAST SALAD

## INGREDIENTS

- 2 handfuls fresh baby arugula or baby kale
- 2 tbsp nutritional yeast
- 2 tbsp olive oil
- 1 handful of cherry tomatoes
- 2 teaspoons freshly-squeezed lemon juice
- cracked black pepper to taste
- pink himalayan salt to taste

## DIRECTIONS

1. Add greens and cherry tomato to a large mixing bowl.
2. Drizzle evenly with olive oil and lemon juice, and sprinkle salt and pepper to taste.
3. Toss until evenly combined. Top with nutritional yeast.
4. Serve immediately and enjoy!

**PREP TIME: 7 MINUTES**
**COOK TIME: 0 MINUTES**
**TOTAL TIME: 7 MINUTES**

# SAVORY BLACK BEAN TOAST

## INGREDIENTS

- 1/2 can of black beans boiled and mashed
- 1 tablespoon water to thin
- 1 tsp garlic powder
- 1 tsp onion powder
- 1 tsp cumin
- salt and pepper to taste
- handful of sliced cherry tomatoes
- 1/2 avocado as a preferred garnish

## DIRECTIONS

1. Combine spices to black bean mash and evenly mix.
2. Spread onto toast of choice.
3. Add on sliced cherry tomatoes and avocado.
4. Enjoy immediately.

**PREP TIME: 2 MINUTES**
**COOK TIME: 10 MINUTES**
**TOTAL TIME: 12 MINUTES**

# HOMEMADE STRAWBERRY JAM

## INGREDIENTS

- 4 1/2 cups fresh strawberries.

- 2 tbsp lemon juice freshly squeezed.

- 1/4 cup of coconut sugar or maple syrup

## DIRECTIONS

1. In a food processor, blend strawberries until you have a puree-like consistency.

2. Pour the strawberry puree in a large non-stick saucepan and cook on medium-high heat.

3. Add coconut sugar and lemon juice and mix until combined.

4. Keep stirring frequently until jam thickens and bubbles are covering the surface (about 12 minutes).

5. Pour jam into a clean jar and let it cool down completely. Then, seal the jar and refrigerate up to 10 days.

**PREP TIME: 5 MINUTES**
**COOK TIME: 20 MINUTES**
**TOTAL TIME: 25 MINUTES**

# SMOOTHIE

# NOMS

# BEAUTY AND THE GREENS SMOOTHIE BOWL

## INGREDIENTS

- 1/2 avocado
- 1 frozen banana
- 1 scoop vanilla protein powder
- 1 cup coconut milk
- 1 handful of spinach
- 1 tsp chia seeds
- 1 1/2 cup of ice
- 1 tsp hemp seeds to garnish
- 1 tsp pumpkin seeds
- berries to garnish

## DIRECTIONS

1. Place all ingredients into blender, leaving the garnishes for the top.
2. Blend until smooth and creamy. Pour into bowl and garnish with berries, pumpkin seeds and hemp seeds.
3. Serve immediately.

**PREP TIME: 5 MINUTES**
**COOK TIME: 0 MINUTES**
**TOTAL TIME: 5 MINUTES**

# THIN MINT CACAO DATE SHAKE

## INGREDIENTS

- 4 dates
- 1 frozen banana
- 1 cup almond or cashew milk
- 1 tbsp fresh mint leaves (or 1-2 drops peppermint oil)
- 1/2 tbsp cacao powder
- 1 1/2 cup of ice

## DIRECTIONS

1. Place all ingredients into blender.
2. Blend until smooth and creamy.
3. Serve immediately.

**PREP TIME: 5 MINUTES**
**COOK TIME: 0 MINUTES**
**TOTAL TIME: 5 MINUTES**

# BERRY BLUE MAJIK SMOOTHIE BOWL

## INGREDIENTS

- 1 cup frozen mango

- 1 cup frozen pineapple

- 1 cup blueberries

- 1 cup ice

- 1 frozen banana

- 1 cup coconut milk

- 1 tsp blue spirulina

- 2 tbsp unsweetened coconut flakes to

  garnish

## DIRECTIONS

1. Combine all ingredients into a blender, leaving a few berries aside to garnish.
2. Blend until smooth and creamy. Pour into bowl and top with garnish. To make swirl design, sprinkle extra spirulina on top and swirl with toothpick.
3. Enjoy immediately.

**PREP TIME: 5 MINUTES**
**COOK TIME: 0 MINUTES**
**TOTAL TIME: 5 MINUTES**

# FROZEN CHOCOLATE MILKSHAKE SMOOTHIE

## INGREDIENTS

- 1 1/4 cups ice
- 2 frozen bananas
- 2 tbsp cacao powder
- 1 cup almond milk

## DIRECTIONS

1. Combine ingredients in a blender.
2. Blend until smooth.
3. Serve and enjoy immediately.

**PREP TIME: 5 MINUTES**
**COOK TIME: 0 MINUTES**
**TOTAL TIME: 5 MINUTES**

# IMMUNITY BOOSTING PINK SMOOTHIE

## INGREDIENTS

- 1 frozen banana
- 1 cup frozen raspberries
- 1 cup frozen pitaya (dragon fruit)
- 1 cup almond milk
- 2 tbsp elderberry syrup
- 1 tsbp chia seeds

## DIRECTIONS

1. Combine ingredients in a blender.
2. Blend until smooth.
3. Serve and enjoy immediately.

**PREP TIME: 5 MINUTES**
**COOK TIME: 0 MINUTES**
**TOTAL TIME: 5 MINUTES**

# CHOCO-COCO HEMP SMOOTHIE

## INGREDIENTS

- 1  frozen banana

- 1 cup almond milk

- 2 tbp hemp seeds

- 1 tbsp cacao powder

- 1/2 can coconut cream

- 1 scoop chocolate protein powder

- unsweetened coconut flakes for garnish

## DIRECTIONS

1. Combine ingredients in a blender, leaving out coconut flakes to garnish.
2. Blend until smooth.
3. Serve and enjoy immediately.

**PREP TIME: 5 MINUTES**
**COOK TIME: 0 MINUTES**
**TOTAL TIME: 5 MINUTES**

# IRON BOOSTING SUNSHINE SMOOTHIE

## INGREDIENTS

- 1 scoop vegan chocolate protein powder
- 1 tbsp cacao
- 2 frozen bananas
- 1 cup spinach
- 4 dates
- 2 tbsp sun butter
- 2 tbsp hemp seeds
- 1 cup almond milk

## DIRECTIONS

1. Combine all ingredients into a blender.
2. Blend until smooth. Pour into bowl or cup.
3. Serve immediately and enjoy!

**PREP TIME: 5 MINUTES**
**COOK TIME: 0 MINUTES**
**TOTAL TIME: 5 MINUTES**

# GREEN GODDESS BLENDED SMOOTHIE

## INGREDIENTS

- 1 handful of baby kale

- 2 handfuls of spinach

- 2 frozen bananas

- 2 cups filtered water

- 2 peeled mandarins

- 3 sliced red apples

- 1 cucumber peeled

- 1 lemon (juiced)

- 1 inch of fresh ginger

## DIRECTIONS

1. Combine ingredients into a blender.
2. Blend until smooth.
3. Serve immediately.

**PREP TIME: 5 MINUTES**
**COOK TIME: 0 MINUTES**
**TOTAL TIME: 5 MINUTES**

# FROZEN CHAI LATTE SMOOTHIE

## INGREDIENTS

- 1 inch fresh ginger
- 1/4 tsp cardamom
- 1 tsp cinnamon
- 1 tsp clove
- 1 tsp vanilla extract
- 1 cup ice
- 1 cup coconut milk
- 1 scoop vanilla protein powder
- 1 cup brewed chai tea
- 4 dates
- 1/2 frozen banana

## DIRECTIONS

1. Combine all ingredients into a blender.
2. Blend until smooth.
3. Serve immediately and enjoy!

**PREP TIME: 5 MINUTES**
**COOK TIME: 0 MINUTES**
**TOTAL TIME: 5 MINUTES**

# SWEET GREEN TROPICAL HEMP SMOOTHIE

## INGREDIENTS

- 2 tbsp hemp seeds
- 1 scoop hemp protein
- 1 cup frozen pineapple
- 1 1/2 cup coconut milk
- 1 handful of spinach
- 2 tbsp shredded coconut
- 1 frozen banana

## DIRECTIONS

1. Combine ingredients into blender.
2. Blend until smooth.
3. Serve immediately.

**PREP TIME: 5 MINUTES**
**COOK TIME: 0 MINUTES**
**TOTAL TIME: 5 MINUTES**

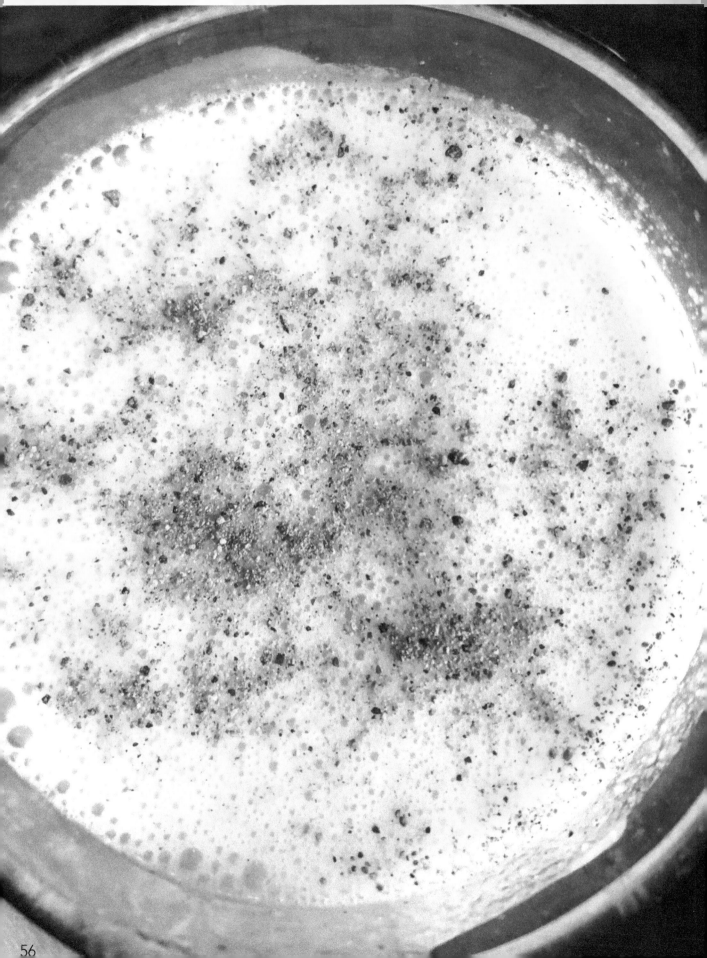

# SPICED PEACHES AND CREAM SMOOTHIE

## INGREDIENTS

- 1 cup frozen peaches
- 1 inch fresh ginger
- 1/4 tsp clove
- 1 tsp vanilla extract
- 1 cup oat milk
- 1/4 tsp nutmeg
- 1/2 frozen banana
- 1 cup ice

## DIRECTIONS

1. Combine ingredients into blender.
2. Blend until smooth.
3. Serve immediately.

**PREP TIME: 5 MINUTES**
**COOK TIME: 0 MINUTES**
**TOTAL TIME: 5 MINUTES**

# LUNCH & DINNER

# NOMS

# WARM SOUL SALAD

## INGREDIENTS

- 1 bunch of kale
- 1/2 cubed avocado
- 1 tbsp lemon juice
- 3 tbsp avocado oil
- salt to taste
- 4 tbsp pumpkin seeds
- 1 tsp garlic powder
- 1 tsp onion powder
- sprinkle of crushed red pepper flakes

## DIRECTIONS

1. Heat the avocado oil in a small-medium fry pan. Add all of the ingredients (minus the avocado) and spices to the pan.
2. Cook for 3-5 minutes, until the kale has softened and crisped up around the edges.
3. Toss with pumpkin seeds and avocado cubes. Best served warm.

**PREP TIME: 5 MINUTES**
**COOK TIME: 15 MINUTES**
**TOTAL TIME: 20 MINUTES**

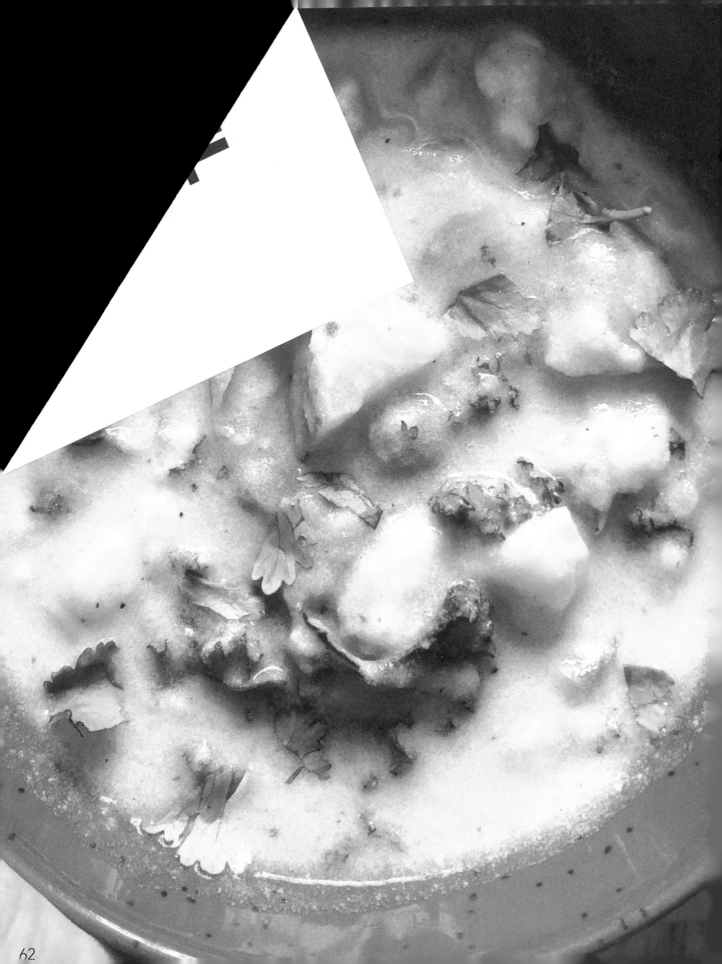

# VEGAN CREAMY POTATO & KALE SOUP

## INGREDIENTS

- 1 container of vegetable broth
- 1 can of full fat coconut milk
- 1/2 small white onion, chopped
- 5 medium golden potatoes, cubed
- 1 tbsp nutritional yeast
- 5 carrots chopped
- 2 cups of chopped kale
- 1 cup of chopped celery
- 2 cloves of garlic chopped finely
- salt and pepper to taste

## DIRECTIONS

1. Chop the onion and sauté it until soft in a medium-sized saucepan.
2. Cut the potatoes into cubes and add them to the pan, along with the broth, coconut milk and spices.
3. Bring to a boil. Then simmer covered, for about 15 minutes.
4. Stir over low heat until veggies and potatoes are soft.
5. Enjoy warm!

**PREP TIME: 5 MINUTES**
**COOK TIME: 35 MINUTES**
**TOTAL TIME: 40 MINUTES**

# MONGOLIAN BBQ "BEEF" & BEAN SALAD

## INGREDIENTS

- 2 cups of chopped romaine
- 1/4 cup of chopped red onion
- 1/4 cup of pinto beans
- 1/2 avocado chopped
- 1 cup of cooked vegan meat crumbles
- 2 tbsp bbq sauce to drizzle for dressing
- 2 tbsp avocado oil
- salt and pepper to taste

## DIRECTIONS

1. Cook vegan meat crumbles (or beef if you eat meat) in saucepan until fully cooked.
2. Add chopped romaine, onion, beans, vegan meat crumbles and avocado to a serving bowl.
3. Drizzle avocado oil and bbq sauce over the salad. Add salt and pepper to taste.
4. Enjoy!

**PREP TIME: 8 MINUTES**
**COOK TIME: 7 MINUTES**
**TOTAL TIME: 15 MINUTES**

# MEDITERRANEAN WRAP W/ VEGAN TZATZIKI SAUCE

## INGREDIENTS

- 1 medium cucumber peeled and chopped
- 1 small tomato diced
- 1/2 red pepper sliced
- 1 1/2 cup vegan yogurt (I used unsweetened coconut)
- 2 tablespoons chopped fresh or dried dill
- 1 clove of garlic minced
- 1 tablespoon lemon juice
- salt and pepper to taste
- large tortillas
- 1/4 cup chickpeas drained and smashed

## DIRECTIONS

1. Peel and chop cucumber. Sprinkle it with a pinch of salt.
2. In a bowl combine the chopped cucumber, vegan yogurt, dill, garlic, lemon juice and a pinch of salt and pepper. Mix well.
3. Make the wraps with a handful of lettuce, smashed chickpeas, tomato, red onion and red pepper with a a few dollops of the tzatziki.
4. Enjoy!

**PREP TIME: 15 MINUTES**
**COOK TIME: 0 MINUTES**
**TOTAL TIME: 15 MINUTES**

# GARLICKY SPICY RAMEN NOODLE SOUP

## INGREDIENTS

- 1 container of veggie broth (chicken broth works well, too)
- 1 package of gluten-free millet brown rice ramen style noodles
- 2 cloves of minced garlic (or 1 tsp garlic powder)
- 1 tsp onion powder
- 1 cup of mushrooms
- 1 cup on spinach
- salt and pepper to taste
- red pepper flakes or cayenne to taste

## DIRECTIONS

1. Place noodles into medium pot with the broth.
2. Bring noodles to a boil. Add in spices, garlic and veggies to the broth. (Any veggies work or you can keep it simply broth and noodles.)
3. Simmer until noodles are done and soft.
4. Enjoy served warm!

**PREP TIME: 5 MINUTES**
**COOK TIME: 15 MINUTES**
**TOTAL TIME: 20 MINUTES**

# VEGAN HIGH PROTEIN MINESTRONE SOUP

## INGREDIENTS

- 1 container of veggie broth
- 1/2 medium white onion chopped
- 1/2 bag frozen peas
- 4 golden potatoes chopped
- 1 can of kidney beans
- 1 can of diced tomatoes
- 3 chopped carrots
- 1 cup chopped celery
- 1 cup spinach
- 1 cup green beans
- 1 package of chickpea pasta shells
- 2 tsp garlic powder or 2 garlic cloves chopped
- salt and pepper to taste
- 1 tsp dried oregano
- 1 tsp dried basil

**PREP TIME: 15 MINUTES**
**COOK TIME: 30 MINUTES**
**TOTAL TIME: 35 MINUTES**

## DIRECTIONS

1. Add broth and soup ingredients (minus the pasta)  to one large pot.
2. Cover soup and bring to a boil. Uncover and reduce to a gentle simmer for 10 minutes.
3. Add pasta and cook just until al dente.
4. Remove from heat and stir in spinach and let wilt.
 Add additional water if desired for a less "chunky" soup.
5. Ladle soup into bowls and serve warm.

# BURRITO BOWL W/ CHILI HONEY LIME DRESSING

## INGREDIENTS

- 2 cups cooked basmati rice
- 1/4 cup cooked can of black beans
- 3 tbsp chopped cilantro
- 1/4 cup salsa
- 1/2 cubed avocado
- 2 tbsp honey
- 1 tsp salt
- 2 tbsp avocado oil
- 1 tbsp chili lime seasoning (or 1 tsp chili powder, 1 pinch cayenne)
- 1 tbsp lime juice
- 1 tsp garlic powder

## DIRECTIONS

1. Scoop rice and beans into a large serving bowl.
2. Add a dollop of salsa, avocado and cilantro.
3. In a separate bowl, add honey, chili lime seasoning, lime juice, spices and avocado oil for dressing.
4. Lightly whisk dressing until evenly mixed.
5. Pour dressing over burrito bowl and enjoy!

**PREP TIME: 7 MINUTES**
**COOK TIME: 15 MINUTES**
**TOTAL TIME: 22 MINUTES**

# VEGAN "CHICK'N" SALAD SANDWICH

## INGREDIENTS

- 1 can of chickpeas, drained and pat dried (works great if chickpeas are smashed, too)
- 1/4 cup chopped white onion
- 1 tsp garlic powder
- 1/4 cup soy-free vegan mayo
- 1/4 cup chopped celery
- salt and pepper to taste
- large tortilla shells

## DIRECTIONS

1. Combine all ingredients into a mixing bowl.
2. Mix ingredients well and chill for 30 minutes or so.
3. Serve "chick'n" salad inside a large GF tortilla shell. This one is grain-free and vegan.
4. Enjoy!

**PREP TIME: 12 MINUTES**
**COOK TIME: 0 MINUTES**
**TOTAL TIME: 12 MINUTES**

# CHEEZY PUMPKIN & MUSHROOM PASTA

## INGREDIENTS

- 1 can pumpkin puree

- 1/2 can full fat coconut milk

- 4 tbsp nutritional yeast

- 1 tbsp soy-free vegan butter

- 1 cup mushrooms

- 1 cup baby kale

- 1 tsp garlic powder

- salt and pepper to taste

- crushed red pepper flakes to taste (I like a bit of spice on mine)

- 1 box of high protein chickpea cavatappi pasta (or brown rice noodles work, too!)

## DIRECTIONS

1. Boil water and cook pasta. Once pasta is cooked, drain and set aside.
2. To make the sauce, add pumpkin puree, garlic, coconut milk. sea salt,  and nutritional yeast in a blender.
3. Blend on high until creamy and smooth.
4. Put baby kale and mushroom into a rimmed skillet with the butter and cook until kale is wilted and mushrooms are softer.
5. Add sauce to the skillet with the vegetables and heat over medium-low heat, stirring frequently until sauce is hot and slightly thickened.
6. To serve, add cooked pasta to the sauce and toss to combine. Serve warm!

**PREP TIME: 10 MINUTES**
**COOK TIME: 35 MINUTES**
**TOTAL TIME: 45 MINUTES**

# GRANDMA KAY'S CHICKEN NOODLE SOUP

## INGREDIENTS

- 1/2 yellow onion chopped
- 2 cloves garlic minced
- 4 stalks celery sliced thinly
- salt and coarse black pepper to taste
- 1 package of brown rice gluten-free noodles
- 2 boneless / skinlesss chicken breast (omit or use vegan meat replacement of choice, like shredded jackfruit)
- 4 large carrots sliced
- 4 cups of chicken broth (to make vegan, use a veggie broth or a vegan chicken broth replacement of choice)

## DIRECTIONS

1. Cook noodles in a separate pot and set aside. (I keep the noodles stored separately to keep them from expanding and getting soggy over night. This way the noodles are still firm for leftovers.)
2. Add veggies, garlic, chopped onion, broth and chicken to a large pot and bring to a boil.
3. Boil until chicken is fully cooked, around 20 minutes.
4. Reduce to simmer and cook until veggies are soft. Stir in the spices and adjust accordingly. If broth gets too low, add more in as it lowers. Adding water may water down the flavor, broth works much better.
5. Take cooked chicken out and shred with two forks before serving into the soup.
5. Add 1-2 scoops of pasta and ladle the soup into a serving bowl. Enjoy warm!

**PREP TIME: 10 MINUTES**
**COOK TIME: 30 MINUTES**
**TOTAL TIME: 40 MINUTES**

# THREE BEAN & POTATO SWEET CHILI

## INGREDIENTS

- 1 package of ground beef, ground turkey or vegan beef crumbles (or omit meat entirely)
- 2 tbsp GF and vegan bbq sauce
- 3-4 tbsp coconut sugar
- 3 tbsp chili powder (sweet paprika, garlic powder, cayenne pepper, onion powder, oregano and cumin)
- 1 onion diced
- 2 medium diced golden potatoes
- 1 jalapeño seeded and finely diced
- 4 cloves garlic minced
- 1 teaspoon cumin
- 1 green bell pepper seeded and diced
- 14.5 oz tomato puree
- 1 19 oz kidney beans canned, drained & rinsed
- 1/2 can pinto beans canned, drained & rinsed
- 1/2 can black beans canned, drained & rinsed
- 14.5 oz diced tomatoes with juice

## DIRECTIONS

1. Combine cooked meat and 1 1/2 tablespoons chili powder.
2. In a large pot place seasoned ground meat, onion, jalapeño, and garlic.
3. In a separate pot, boil diced potatoes until soft.
4. Add in remaining ingredients and bring to a boil.
5. Reduce heat and simmer uncovered 45-60 minutes or until chili has reached desired thickness. Adjust seasonings as necessary.
6. Top with vegan cheese or nutritional yeast, green onions, cilantro or your other favorite toppings.

**PREP TIME: 30 MINUTES**
**COOK TIME: 20 MINUTES**
**TOTAL TIME: 50 MINUTES**

# COCONUT CURRY SPICED CHICKEN AND RICE SOUP

## INGREDIENTS

- 1 can of full fat coconut milk
- 2 tbsp nutritional yeast
- 2 tsp curry powder
- 2 boneless/skinless chicken breast or vegan meat replacement of choice, like shredded jackfruit
- 2 cups cooked basmati rice
- 1 1/2 containers of veggie broth
- 2 diced medium gold potatoes
- 3 large carrots chopped
- 1/2 onion chopped
- 1 1/2 cup frozen peas
- 1 tsp garlic powder
- 1 tsp onion powder
- pinch of ginger powder
- salt and cracked black pepper to taste

**PREP TIME: 30 MINUTES**
**COOK TIME: 30 MINUTES**
**TOTAL TIME: 1 HOUR**

## DIRECTIONS

1. Boil and shred chicken. Set aside.
2. In a separate pot, cook basmati rice until done. Set aside.
3. In a large stew pot, add the coconut milk, broth, onion, veggies and spices. Bring to a boil and reduce to a simmer.
4. Simmer until veggies are soft. Add spices, chicken and rice to the pot.
5. Serve immediately.

# VEGAN FETTUCINE ALFREDO PASTA

## INGREDIENTS

- 1 can full fat coconut milk
- 1 package of mushrooms
- 1/2 white onion diced
- 2 tbsp of soy-free vegan butter
- 2 tbsp coconut aminos
- 1 box gluten-free brown rice fettuccine noodles
- 1 tbsp gluten-free all purpose flour
- 1 tsp garlic powder
- 1 tsp onion powder
- 1 tbsp oregano
- salt and pepper to taste
- 1/2 cup vegan cream cheese alternative (I used one with an almond base)
- optional: vegan parmesan cheese

## DIRECTIONS

1. Cook fettuccine noodles and set aside.

2. To make the alfredo sauce, cook the mushrooms and onions down into the butter base on medium heat in a large saucepan.

3. Add coconut milk, coconut aminos, spices, cream cheese, and other ingredients into a high powered blender or food processor. Blend until smooth and thick.

4. Pour sauce into saucepan with mushrooms and onion and simmer. Add the noodles in and stir gently.

6. Serve immediately and top with vegan parmesan cheese.

**PREP TIME: 20 MINUTES**
**COOK TIME: 30 MINUTES**
**TOTAL TIME: 50 MINUTES**

# LEMON VEGETABLE QUINOA BOWL

## INGREDIENTS

- 2 cups cooked quiona
- 2 tbsp avocado oil
- 1/4 cup cooked pinto beans
- 1 sweet potato cubed
- 1 bunch of broccoli
- 1/2 white onion
- 2 tbsp lemon juice
- 3 cups of vegetable broth
- 1 tsp garlic powder
- salt and pepper to taste

## DIRECTIONS

1. Cook quinoa in the 3 cups of vegetable broth for extra flavor in a separate pot and set aside. Cook pinto beans on low and also set aside.
2. In a large saucepan with avocado oil, cook the broccoli, sweet potatoes and spices.
3. In a serving bowl, scoop quinoa, pinto bean and cooked potato and broccoli medley. Drizzle over lemon juice.
4. Enjoy warm or cold.

**PREP TIME: 5 MINUTES**
**COOK TIME: 20 MINUTES**
**TOTAL TIME: 25 MINUTES**

# SPICY ORANGE CHICKEN STIR FRY

## INGREDIENTS

- 2 cups cooked basmati rice
- 1 red pepper sliced into strips
- 1/2 white onion chopped
- 1/2 green pepper sliced into strips
- 1 bunch of fresh or frozen broccoli
- 1 bunch of fresh or frozen cauliflower
- 1 tsp garlic powder
- 2 tbsp avocado oil
- salt and pepper to taste
- 4 tbsp coconut aminos
- 1 cup orange juice
- 1/4 cup coconut sugar
- 4 tbsp bbq sauce
- cayenne to taste (if you like it spicy, add more)
- 2 chicken breasts cubed and cooked (or use jackfruit or hempeh to make vegan)

**PREP TIME: 15 MINUTES**
**COOK TIME: 45 MINUTES**
**TOTAL TIME: 1 HOUR**

## DIRECTIONS

1. Cook the basmati rice in a separate pot and set aside.
2. Cook chicken or tofu with the veggies and onion in a large pan with avocado oil. Cook on medium-high until chicken is cooked through and veggies are softer, but still slightly crunchy.
3. While you cook the protein and veggies, pour orange juice, coconut aminos, bbq sauce, spices and bbq into a mixing bowl. Whisk until sauce is evenly mixed and thick. Set aside.
4. Pour the sauce over the veggies and protein. Stir to evenly coat veggies.
5. Scoop rice onto serving plate and top with the orange chicken veggie mix.
6. Serve warm!

# VEGAN TOMATO, MUSHROOM & KALE CREAM SAUCE

## INGREDIENTS

- 1/2 can full fat coconut milk
- 4 tbsp tomato sauce
- 2 tbsp extra virgin olive oil
- 1 package crimini mushrooms
- 1 cup cherry tomatoes
- 1/2 white onion diced
- 2 tbsp coconut aminos
- 2 tbsp nutritional yeast
- 2 cups baby kale
- crushed red pepper to taste (I also like spicy)
- 1 tsp garlic powder
- 1 tsp oregano
- 1 tsp basil
- salt and pepper to taste
- 1 box of gluten-free  brown rice or chickpea penne pasta

**PREP TIME: 15 MINUTES**
**COOK TIME: 45 MINUTES**
**TOTAL TIME: 1 HOUR**

## DIRECTIONS

1. Put veggies and onion in a medium pan. Add olive oil and cook until kale is wilted. Set aside.
2. Cook gluten-free penne pasta in separate pot and set aside.
3. In a separate pan, pour coconut milk, tomato sauce, spices, coconut aminos and nutritional yeast. Cook on medium-high heat and reduce to a simmer. Stir frequently until cream sauce thickens up a bit.
4. Add veggies to the cream sauce. Stir in the penne pasta.
5, Serve warm with fresh vegan parmesean and basil on top.

# NUT-FREE PUMPKIN SEED PESTO PASTA

## INGREDIENTS

- 1 package gluten-free brown rice noodles
- 1 large bunch basil
- 1/2 large bunch parsley
- 3 garlic cloves
- 2 tbsp lemon juice
- 3/4 cup olive oil
- 1/4 tsp sea salt
- 4 tbsp pumpkin seeds
- 3 tbsp nutritional yeast or vegan parmesean

## DIRECTIONS

1. In a food processor, blend parsley, lemon juice, olive oil, pumpkin seeds, nutritional yeast, basil, salt and garlic. This is your nut-free pesto sauce.
2. Cook gluten-free pasta in a separate pot, strain and set aside.
3. In a large mixing bowl, pour pesto sauce and chopped cherry tomatoes over the pasta.
4. Served warm or chilled as a summertime or holiday pasta salad.

**PREP TIME: 20 MINUTES**
**COOK TIME: 15 MINUTES**
**TOTAL TIME: 35 MINUTES**

# DAIRY-FREE & GLUTEN-FREE ENCHILADAS

## INGREDIENTS

- 8-12 gluten-free tortilla shells
- 1 package dairy-free cheese shreds
- 1 can tomato paste
- 1 can pinto beans
- 1 package ground turkey, beef or vegan meat crumbles
- 2 tsp chili powder
- 1 tsp garlic powder
- 1 tsp onion powder
- 1 tsp salt
- 1 tsp cayenne pepper
- 1 tsp cumin powder
- 1/2 white onion chopped
- 1 jalapeño chopped

## DIRECTIONS

1. Preheat oven to 350.
2. In a large skillet, brown the ground beef and chopped onions over medium-high heat. Drain the excess fat away and return the meat to the skillet and to medium-low heat. OR cook the vegan meat crumbles until done. Stir in 1 can of pinto beans to the meat mixture.
3. In a separate pot, pour in tomato paste. Slowly stir while adding water. Sauce should be thin enough to pour, but not too watery. Add in spices and cook on medium heat until thin and warm. Add half of this enchilada sauce to the meat and bean mixture. Then mix until sauce is coated evenly.
4. Pour about 4 tbsp of the enchilada sauce in the bottom of the prepared baking dish. Line the tortillas with the centers of the shells open. Add about 1/4 cup of the meat mixture down the center of each tortilla and top with about 1 heaping tablespoon of cheese.
5.. Tightly roll each tortilla up and place them in the dish, seam side down. Pour the remaining enchilada sauce over them and sprinkle the remaining cheese over.
6. Bake for 30 to 35 minutes. Serve warm with sliced jalapeño peppers.

**PREP TIME: 20 MINUTES**
**COOK TIME: 25 MINUTES**
**TOTAL TIME: 45 MINUTES**

# CREAMY CURRY VEGGIE STIRFRY

## INGREDIENTS

- 1/2 can of full fat coconut milk
- 1 tsp garlic
- 1 tsp curry powder
- 1/2 tsp cayenne (optional but recommend if you like spicy!)
- salt and pepper to taste
- 1/2 tsp onion powder
- 1 bag frozen broccoli
- 1 red bell pepper sliced
- 1/2 white onion sliced in strips
- 1 yellow bell pepper sliced
- 1/2 zucchini chopped
- 1 package of mushrooms
- 1 tbsp coconut aminos
- 2 tbsp avocado oil

## DIRECTIONS

1. Combine veggies with oil in a large stir fry pan.
2. Simmer veggies, mushrooms and onions until mostly soft.
3. Add coconut milk, coconut aminos and spices. Cook until sauce is bubbling with heat, then reduce to a simmer. Cook until sauce is warm and beings to thicken. If you like a thicker sauce, feel free to add a little slurry to thicken it (whisk 1 tbsp of rice flour and water to make a "slurry" thickener. Make sure to whisk out all clumps before adding in the slurry)
4. Serve over basmati rice, brown rice noodles or add in a protein of choice. Enjoy warm!

**PREP TIME: 10 MINUTES**
**COOK TIME: 20 MINUTES**
**TOTAL TIME: 30 MINUTES**

# BEVERAGE

# NOMS

# DIY BLUE ELECTROLYTE DRINK

## INGREDIENTS

- 1/2 cup lime juice
- 1 1/3 cup of filtered water
- 1/8 tsp pink himalayan salt
- 2 tbsp honey of sweetener or choice (stevia works as well for a zero calorie and zero sugar option)
- 1/2 tsp blue spirulina (for natural blue hue)

## DIRECTIONS

1. Combine all ingredients in a mason jar. Lightly stir salt and honey in until evenly mixed. Or shake vigorously with a sealed lid.
2. Serve chilled or with ice.

**PREP TIME: 2 MINUTES**
**COOK TIME: 0 MINUTES**
**TOTAL TIME: 2 MINUTES**

# FRUITY WINE SLUSHIE

## INGREDIENTS

- 1/2 bag of frozen strawberries
- 1/2 bottle of rosé wine
- 1/2 bag of frozen peaches

## DIRECTIONS

1. Combine into a high powered blender.
2. Blend until smooth.
3. Serve immediately in wine glasses.

**PREP TIME: 3 MINUTES**
**COOK TIME: 0 MINUTES**
**TOTAL TIME: 3 MINUTES**

# ALKALINE LEMONADE

## INGREDIENTS

- 4 tbsp lemon juice
- 1 tsp green algae or spirulina
- 2 tbsp honey or sweetener of choice
- 1 1/2 cup filtered water

## DIRECTIONS

1. Combine ingredients into a mason jar.
2. Lightly stir honey in until evenly mixed. Or shake vigorously with a sealed lid.
3. Serve chilled or with ice.

**PREP TIME: 2 MINUTES**
**COOK TIME: 0 MINUTES**
**TOTAL TIME: 2 MINUTES**

# LAVENDER LONDON FOG LATTE

## INGREDIENTS

- 1 cup earl grey tea

- 1 tbsp honey

- 1 cup oat milk

- 1/4 tsp vanilla extract

- 1/4 tsp food grade lavender

- (1/2 drop of food grade lavender oil

  works as well. It's much stronger, so use

  a VERY small amount!)

## DIRECTIONS

1. Steep one cup of earl grey tea and honey in a separate mug.
2. Add oat milk, lavender and vanilla extract to a saucepan and heat until warm but not boiling.
3. Pour lavender milk into separate mug. Use a milk frother to make milk foam or add milk to a high powered blender for one minute to create froth.
4. Pour milk froth on top of earl grey tea. Garnish with fresh dried lavender & enjoy warm,

**PREP TIME: 5 MINUTES**
**COOK TIME: 7 MINUTES**
**TOTAL TIME: 12 MINUTES**

# TENSION TAMER TURMERIC LATTE

## INGREDIENTS

- 1 1/2 cup plant milk of choice
- 1 tsp turmeric powder
- 1/4 tsp cinnamon
- pinch of black pepper
- 1 tbsp maple syrup
- 1 serving of unflavored CBD oil (optional but reccomended)

## DIRECTIONS

1. Combine ingredients into blender. Blend for 30 seconds.
2. Pour into mug over ice.
3. Enjoy immediately!

**PREP TIME: 5 MINUTES**
**COOK TIME: 0 MINUTES**
**TOTAL TIME: 5 MINUTES**

# CAT'S PAJAMA'S SLEEPY TIME COCKTAIL

## INGREDIENTS

- 1 cup of 100% cherry juice
- 1 dropper of chamomile tincture or 1/2 cup of steeped chamomile tea
- 1 serving unflavored CBD oil
- (optional 2-4 ounces of red wine)

## DIRECTIONS

1. Combine all ingredients in cup of choice. Stir lightly.
2. Can be served warm, room temperature or chilled.

**PREP TIME: 5 MINUTES**
**COOK TIME: 0 MINUTES**
**TOTAL TIME: 5 MINUTES**

# CINNAMON MATCHA LATTE

## INGREDIENTS

- 1/4 tsp cinnamon
- 1 tbsp maple syrup
- 1/2 tsp vanilla extract
- 1/2 cup hot water
- 1 tsp matcha powder
- 1/2 cup plant milk

## DIRECTIONS

1. Combine ingredients into a mug and mix well with a milk frother or blend in a high powered blender. You want to make sure there are no matcha clumps after mixing or blending.
2. Pour into a mug. Dust a little cinnamon on top. Enjoy warm.

**PREP TIME: 5 MINUTES**
**COOK TIME: 0 MINUTES**
**TOTAL TIME: 5 MINUTES**

# HEALTHIER PUMPKIN SPICE LATTE

## INGREDIENTS

- 8 ounces brewed organic coffee
- 1/2 cup oat milk
- 2 tbsp full fat coconut cream
- 4 tbsp pumpkin puree
- 1/2 tsp pumpkin pie spice
- 1/2 tsp vanilla
- 1 tbsp maple syrup
- 1/2 tsp cinnamon

## DIRECTIONS

1. In a sauce pan, mix together oat milk, spices, coconut cream and pumpkin. Cook on medium heat on the stove top until warm.
2. Pour in cup and use a frother or blend for 1 minute to foam the milk.
3. Pour coffee into a large mug, add the foamy milk mixture on top. Sprinkle with cinnamon and enjoy!

**PREP TIME: 5 MINUTES**
**COOK TIME: 5 MINUTES**
**TOTAL TIME: 10 MINUTES**

# DIRTY CHAI COCONUT LATTE

## INGREDIENTS

- 4 oz brewed organic coffee

- 1 cup steeped chai tea

- 2 tbsp full fat coconut cream

- 1 tbsp maple syrup

- 1/4 tsp cinnamon

- 1/4 tsp cardamom

- 1/4 tsp nutmeg

- 1/4 ginger

## DIRECTIONS

1. Combine ingredients into a mug and mix well with a milk frother or blend in a high powered blender.
2. Pour into a mug. Dust a little cinnamon on top.
3. Enjoy warm!

**PREP TIME: 5 MINUTES**
**COOK TIME: 5 MINUTES**
**TOTAL TIME: 10 MINUTES**

# FROTHY VANILLA CARADMOM ROSE LATTE

## INGREDIENTS

- 1/8 tsp vanilla extract
- 1/4 tsp rose extract
- 1 cup of almond milk
- 1 tbsp honey
- 1 cup brewed organic coffee
- 1/4 tsp cardamom

## DIRECTIONS

1. Combine ingredients into a mug and mix well with a milk frother or blend in a high powered blender.
2. Pour into a mug. Dust a little cinnamon on top.
3. Enjoy warm!

**PREP TIME: 5 MINUTES**
**COOK TIME: 5 MINUTES**
**TOTAL TIME: 10 MINUTES**

# ICED MAPLE COFFEE

## INGREDIENTS

- 4 coffee ice cubes
- 1 1/2 cup plant milk of choice
- 1 tbsp maple syrup
- 1 cup cold brew or iced coffee

## DIRECTIONS

1. Freeze coffee into ice cube container overnight. (Great way to make use of leftover coffee!)
2. Add 4 coffee ice cubes to a cup with maple syrup, cold brew coffee and milk.
3, Enjoy immediately.

**PREP TIME: 5 MINUTES**
**COOK TIME: 0 MINUTES**
**TOTAL TIME: 5 MINUTES**

# PINK STRAWBERRY REFRESH DRINK

## INGREDIENTS

- 1 cup steeped hibiscus "passion" tea
- 1 tsp lemon juice
- 1 -2 drops of vanilla stevia extract
- 1 cup frozen strawberries
- 1/2 cup  unsweetened coconut creamer

## DIRECTIONS

1. Combine tea with lemon juice, stevia, and coconut creamer in a large cup. Stir and mix well.
2. Add frozen strawberries as ice cubes.
3. Serve and enjoy immediately!

**PREP TIME: 7 MINUTES**
**COOK TIME: 0 MINUTES**
**TOTAL TIME: 7 MINUTES**

# 5 MINUTE HOMEMADE CHOCOLATE HEMP MYLK

## INGREDIENTS

- 1 cup hemp seeds
- 4 cups filtered water
- 4 pitted dates
- pinch of sea salt
- 2 tbsp cacao powder
- 2 tsp vanilla extract

## DIRECTIONS

1. Combine  ingredients into blender. Blend on high for 1 minute.
2. Use a  flour sifter as a strainer (or nut milk bag) and a large mixing bowl to strain residual seeds and date out of the milk, leaving behind only the creamy mylk.
3. Store in fridge for 3-5 days. Enjoy chilled!

**PREP TIME: 5 MINUTES**
**COOK TIME: 0 MINUTES**
**TOTAL TIME: 5 MINUTES**

# HOLIDAY

# NOMS

# HEALTHY HOMEMADE CRANBERRY SAUCE

## INGREDIENTS

- 1 bag of frozen cranberries
- 3/4 cup of maple syrup
- 1 cup unsweetened apple sauce
- pinch of cinnamon

## DIRECTIONS

1. Combine all ingredients in a medium sauce pan and bring to a boil.
2. Once the sauce bubbles and boils, the cranberries will "pop" open. Turn down to low and cook 10-15 minutes, until thick, stirring frequently and smashing with a spoon.
3. Refrigerate until cold.
4. Serve chilled.

**PREP TIME: 0 MINUTES**
**COOK TIME: 15 MINUTES**
**TOTAL TIME: 15 MINUTES**

# MAMA'S HOMEMADE PAN FRIED RICE CAKES

## INGREDIENTS

- 3 cups cooked short-grain rice
- 2 large eggs, lightly beaten (or 2 flax eggs)
- salt and pepper to taste
- 1 tsp garlic powder
- 1 tsp onion powder
- 1/2 tsp oregano
- 1/2 tsp basil
- 3 tbsp avocado oil
- 1/2 cup peas
- 1/2 cup corn
- 1/4 cup scallions
- 1 tbsp nutritional yeast

## DIRECTIONS

1. In a medium bowl, using your hands, mix together rice, egg, salt, pepper, and scallions. Form into 6 patties. Cover and refrigerate for 30 minutes.
2. In a large skillet over medium-high heat, heat the oil until simmering. Carefully add patties to oil and fry for about 5 minutes on each side, or until golden and crisp.
3. Serve warm with a dipping sauce of choice. (2 tbsp vegan mayo, 1 tsp hot sauce, 1 tsp garlic powder and 1/4 tsp of lemon juice makes a great dipping sauce!)

**PREP TIME: 15 MINUTES**
**COOK TIME: 30 MINUTES**
**TOTAL TIME: 45 MINUTES**

# GF/DF/SF PUMPKIN PIE

## INGREDIENTS

- 1 can pumpkin puree
- 1/4 cup maple syrup
- 1/4 cup coconut sugar
- 1 cup full fat coconut milk
- 1 tbsp avocado oil or coconut oil
- 2 1/2 tbsp arrowroot powder
- 1 tbsp pumpkin pie spice (or sub mix of ginger, cinnamon, nutmeg & cloves)
- 1/4 tsp sea salt
- 1 tsp vanilla extract
- pumpkin pie crust

## DIRECTIONS

1. Preheat oven to 350 F. Add all pie ingredients to a blender and blend until smooth. Taste and adjust seasonings and sweetness as needed. Set aside.

2. Pour filling into pie crust (store bought GF/SF/DF works great or feel free to make your own) and bake for 60-65 minutes. The crust should be light golden brown and the filling will be a bit jiggly and have some cracks on the top. Remove from oven and let cool completely before loosely covering and placing in the refrigerator to fully set preferably overnight.

3. Slice and serve with vegan whipped cream and an additional sprinkle of cinnamon, Enjoy!

**PREP TIME: 15 MINUTES**
**COOK TIME: 1 HOUR**
**TOTAL TIME: 1 HOUR 15 MINUTES**

# CRISPY ROASTED ROSEMARY POTATOES

## INGREDIENTS

- 1 1/2 lbs baby potatoes sliced into thin circles
- 2 tbsp rosemary
- 2-3 tbsp avocado oil
- 1 tsp sea salt

## DIRECTIONS

1. Preheat oven to 425 degrees Fahrenheit. Wash and pat dry potatoes. For a more crispy potato, try soaking in ice water for 20-30 minutes before patting completely dry.

2. Cut potatoes in circles (like potato chips lengthwise) and dry them again. This is so the potatoes roast and not steam.

3. Place in a large mixing bowl and toss with avocado oil, rosemary, and sea salt. Spread potatoes evenly on a baking pan and roast for 35 minutes or until potatoes are tender and cooked through.

4. Remove from oven and allow to rest for 5 minutes before tossing them one last time. Garnish with fresh rosemary, if desired. Enjoy!

**PREP TIME: 15 MINUTES**
**COOK TIME: 35 MINUTES**
**TOTAL TIME: 50 MINUTES**

# VEGAN QUESO CHEEZE DIP

## INGREDIENTS

- 2 medium yellow potatoes
- 1/2 large sweet potato
- 2 carrots
- 1 diced jalapeño or 1 small can of green chiles
- 5 tbsp nutritional yeast
- 2 tbsp salsa of choice
- 1 tsp garlic powder
- 1/2 tsp chili powder
- 1/4 tsp onion powder
- salt to taste

## DIRECTIONS

1. In a large pot, bring potatoes and carrots to a boil. Boil until fully tender and soft.
2. Transfer potatoes and carrots into a food processor or blender with spices, salsa, diced pepper and blend until silky smooth and cheesy. Adjust spices and flavor as needed.
3. Enjoy warm! Store up to 2-5 days. Best served warm with chips of choice.

**PREP TIME: 10 MINUTES**
**COOK TIME: 20 MINUTES**
**TOTAL TIME: 30 MINUTES**

# HONEY BUTTER GLAZED CARROTS

## INGREDIENTS

- 6 carrots cut into long strips
- 2 tbsp vegan butter flavor coconut oil or soy-free vegan butter
- 2 tbsp honey (you can do maple syrup if you wish)
- pink Himalayan salt or flakey sea salt

## DIRECTIONS

1. Combine carrots, melted butter/oil and honey into a large mixing bowl, stirring the mixture to coat carrots.
2. Place carrots into a saucepan and cook until slightly tender and browned, leaving a bit of crunch to them. Dust with salt.
3. Serve immediately and enjoy!

**PREP TIME: 10 MINUTES**
**COOK TIME: 20 MINUTES**
**TOTAL TIME: 30 MINUTES**

# GF/DF STUFFING

## INGREDIENTS

- 1 large loaf gluten-free vegan bread cubed and set out to dry overnight or baked at 375 F for 5-10 minutes
- 1/2 cup vegan soy-free butter
- 1/2 diced white onions
- 1/2 cup diced celery
- salt and pepper to taste
- 3 1/2 cups vegetable broth
- 1 batch flax egg (1 tbsp flaxseed meal + 2 1/2 tbsp water) or 1 real egg if not vegan
- 3/4 tsp dried sage
- 3/4 tsp dried oregano
- 1 tsp garlic powder
- 1 tbsp thyme
- 1 tsp maple syrup

## DIRECTIONS

1. Preheat oven to 350 degrees F and grease a 9x13 pan (or comparable sized dish) Also prepare flax egg and set aside.
2. Sauté onion and celery in vegan butter and season with garlic, salt and pepper. Cook until onions are soft and translucent. Set aside.
3. Pour most of the broth then add the remaining ingredients (sage, cooked veggies, flax egg) over the bread in a large bowl and mix with a wooden spoon. (If it's too dry, add more broth and mix evenly. If it's too wet, add more bread)
4. Transfer to pan and bake for 45 minutes or until top is crispy and golden brown.
5. Remove from oven and serve warm.

**PREP TIME: 15 MINIUTES**
**COOK TIME: 50 MINUTES**
**TOTAL TIME: 1 HOUR 5 MINUTES**

# GRANDMA KAY'S POTATO SALAD

## INGREDIENTS

- 9 cups peeled yukon gold potatoes, chopped in 1 inch chunks
- 1/2 red onion, finely chopped
- 1 cup celery, chopped
- 1 cup vegan soy-free mayo
- 2 tbsp spicy brown mustard
- 1/2 tsp garlic powder
- salt and pepper to taste
- 1 tsp apple cider vinegar
- 1/4 tsp dried dill

## DIRECTIONS

1. Add the chopped potatoes to a large pot and cover them with water. Boil and cook for 10-15 minutes, until the potatoes are tender when pierced with a fork, but not too hard or too mushy.
2. Drain the potatoes. In a large bowl, add the potatoes, onion, celery, spices, mustard, acv and vegan mayo. Mix gently until well combined with a spoon.
3. Cover and refrigerate for a few hours. Best served chilled.

**PREP TIME: 20 MINUTES**
**COOK TIME: 15 MINUTES**
**TOTAL TIME: 35 MINUTES**

# LEMON GARLIC HUMMUS

## INGREDIENTS

- 1 can of chickpeas, drained
- juice from one whole lemon
- salt to taste
- 1/2 tsp smoked paprika
- 2 cloves of fresh garlic
- 1/2 cup tahini

## DIRECTIONS

1. Combine all ingredients into food processor or high powered blender.
2. Blend until smooth and creamy.
3. Pour into serving bowl. Serve immediately or chilled. Best with veggies, pita bread or tortilla chips.

**PREP TIME: 10 MINUTES**
**COOK TIME: 0 MINUTES**
**TOTAL TIME: 10 MINUTES**

# LEMON, GARLIC, DILL TAHINI KALE SALAD

## INGREDIENTS

- 1 large bunch of leafy kale
- 2 tbsp nutritional yeast
- 3 tbsp avocado oil
- 1/4 red onion chopped
- 1 handful of cherry tomatoes
- 1/2 cucumber peeled and chopped
- 1/4 cup pumpkin seeds
- the juice of 1/2 freshly-squeezed lemon
- cracked black pepper
- sea salt to taste
- 1/3 cup tahini
- 2 tsp dried or fresh dill
- 1 tsp garlic powder
- 1/2 tsp smoked paprika
- 3 tbsp of water

**PREP TIME: 7 MIN**
**COOK TIME: 0 MIN**
**TOTAL TIME: 7 MIN**

## DIRECTIONS

1. Add kale to a large mixing bowl with avocado oil. Massage kale for 1-3 minutes, or until kale breakdowns a bit softer. This makes is easier to chew and digest.
2. Add tomatoes, cucumber, onions and pumpkin seeds to the bowl of kale.
3. In a separate bowl, whisk together the dressing: lemon juice, tahini, spices and water. Adding more water or lemon juice if you desire a thinner dressing.
4. Pour salad dressing over salad and toss until evenly combined. Serve immediately. Enjoy!

# SWEET

# NOMS

# FREEZER CHOCOLATE ALMOND BUTTER CUPS

## INGREDIENTS

- 1 cup almond butter
- 1 tbsp maple syrup
- pinch of salt
- 2 tbsp melted coconut oil
- 1/2 cup vegan chocolate chips

## DIRECTIONS

1. Mix almond butter, maple syrup and salt together in a bowl.
2. Spoon out the almond butter mix to the bottoms of cupcake wrappers until they are approximately 1/2 - 2/3 full.
3. Put them in the freezer for at least 15 minutes, or until slightly hardened.
4. In a separate pot, melt vegan chocolate chips and coconut oil.
5. Remove the almond butter cups from the freezer and place 1-2 spoonfuls of the chocolate topping on top of each almond butter cup. Return the almond butter cups back to the freezer for about 30-60 minutes, or until they are hardened.
6. Keep in the freezer until ready to serve because they will melt at room temperature. Enjoy!

**PREP TIME: 10 MINUTES**
**COOK TIME: 0 MINUTES**
**TOTAL TIME: 10 MINUTES**

# CHEWY SOFT BAKED CHOCOLATE CHIP COOKIES

## INGREDIENTS

- 1 1/2 cup GF all purpose flour

- 1/4 tsp salt

- 1 tsp vanilla extract

- 1/4 cup plant milk

- 1/4 cup apple sauce

- 1 tbsp ground flax

- 1/4 tsp baking powder

- 1/4 tsp baking soda

- 1/2 cup coconut sugar

- 1 vegan egg ( 1:1 egg replacer or 1 flax egg) or 1 real egg

- 1/2 cup vegan butter flavor coconut oil or avocado oil

## DIRECTIONS

1. In one bowl, mix together all ingredients. Stir until dough is evenly mixed. Preheat oven to 350.
2. Roll dough into balls, but slightly flatten them out on a baking sheet so they don't rise too high.
3. Bake for 10-12 minutes, or until golden brown.
4. Allow them to cool and enjoy!

**PREP TIME: 5 MINUTES**
**COOK TIME: 10 MINUTES**
**TOTAL TIME: 15 MINUTES**

# VEGAN BANANA CHAI SPICE MUFFUNS

## INGREDIENTS

- 2 spotty bananas
- 2 cups oat flour
- 1/4 cup avocado oil
- 1/3 cup coconut sugar
- 1/2 tsp baking soda
- 1 and 1/2 tsp baking powder
- 1 tsp cinnamon
- 1/4 tsp all spice
- 1/4 tsp cardamom
- 1/4 tsp nutmeg
- 1/4 tsp ginger
- 1 tsp vanilla extract
- 1/2 cup plant milk of choice
- 2 tbsp flax seeds

## DIRECTIONS

1. Preheat oven to 350 F. Combine wet and dry ingredients into a mixing bowl.
2. Mix batter evenly. With ice cream scooper, scoop out batter into muffin pan.
3. Place muffin pan in oven and cook for 25 minutes or until tops are golden brown and a toothpick comes out clean.
4. Let cool before serving. Enjoy!

**PREP TIME: 10 MINUTES**
**COOK TIME: 25 MINUTES**
**TOTAL TIME: 35 MINUTES**

# STRAWBERRY MELON SORBET

## INGREDIENTS

- 4 cups frozen watermelon
- 3 frozen bananas
- 2 cups frozen strawberries
- 1 container almond milk greek style yogurt
- oat milk (to thin while blending)
- juice from 1 lemon

## DIRECTIONS

1. Combine all ingredients in a high powered blender and blend until smooth.
2. Pour sorbet contents into a baking dish or storage container of choice.
3. Freeze until solid.
4. Before serving, let sit at room temperature for about 15-20 minutes and scoop like sorbet. Enjoy!

**PREP TIME: 10 MINUTES**
**COOK TIME: 45 MINUTES**
**TOTAL TIME: 1 HOUR**

# 2 MINUTE DOUBLE CHOCOLATE MUG CAKE

## INGREDIENTS

- 1/2 ripe spotty banana mashed very well
- 2 tbsp plant milk
- 2 tbsp vegan chocolate chips
- 2 tbsp melted vegan soy-free butter or vegan butter flavor coconut oil
- 1/4 tsp baking powder
- 1 tsp cacao powder
- 1 tsp cocoa powder
- 2 tbsp coconut sugar or maple syrup
- 1/4 cup oat flour
- 1 tsp vanilla extract
- pinch of salt

## DIRECTIONS

1. Combine all ingredients in a mixing bowl and mix until batter is smooth.
2. Scoop batter into a mug or mini ceramic bowl.
3. Microwave for 2 minutes.
4. Let cool and use oven mitt before removing if the mug or bowl doesn't have a handle, the cake gets pretty hot. Enjoy warm while chocolate chips are still melty.

**PREP TIME: 5 MINUTES**
**COOK TIME: 2 MINUTES**
**TOTAL TIME: 7 MINUTES**

# PUMPKIN SPICE MUG CAKE

## INGREDIENTS

- 2 tbsp plant milk
- 1/4 cup pumpkin puree
- 2 tbsp vegan chocolate chips (optional)
- 1 tbsp avocado oil
- 1/4 tsp baking powder
- 1 tsp pumpkin spice
- 1/4 tsp cinnamon
- 2 tbsp coconut sugar or maple syrup
- 1/4 cup oat flour
- 1 tsp vanilla extract
- pinch of salt

## DIRECTIONS

1. Combine all ingredients in a mixing bowl and mix until batter is smooth.
2. Scoop batter into a mug or mini ceramic bowl.
3. Microwave for 2-3 minutes.
4. Let cool and use oven mitt before removing if the mug or bowl doesn't have a handle, the cake gets pretty hot. Enjoy warm .

**PREP TIME: 5 MINUTES**
**COOK TIME: 2 MINUTES**
**TOTAL TIME: 7 MINUTES**

# VEGAN STRAWBERRY SINGLE LAYER CAKE

## INGREDIENTS

- 1 cup strawberry puree (use 1 pint of fresh strawberries)
- 1 tbsp natural red coloring (freeze dried strawberry powder, pomegranate or beet powder work well)
- 2 vegan eggs (1:1 egg replacer or 2 flax eggs)
- 1 tbsp apple cider vinegar
- 1 cup coconut milk
- 2 cups oat flour
- 1 cup coconut sugar
- 1 tsp baking soda
- 1 tsp lemon juice
- 1 tsp baking powder
- 1/2 tsp salt
- 1/2 cup vegan butter flavor coconut oil, melted
- 2 tsp strawberry extract
- fresh blueberries and sliced strawberries for garnishing

**PREP TIME: 25 MINUTES**
**COOK TIME: 35 MINUTES**
**TOTAL TIME: 1 HOUR**

## DIRECTIONS

1. Make the strawberry puree: Add the fresh strawberries to a blender and blend until small pieces remain. Make the vegan buttermilk: Pour 1 tbsp apple cider vinegar into a 1 cup measuring cup and fill the remaining cup with coconut milk.

2. Grease and lightly flour 1 9 inch round cake pan. Set both aside.

3. Preheat your oven to 350 degrees. In a large bowl, add the flour, sugar, salt, baking soda, and baking powder. Whisk together. Fold in melted oil, strawberry extract and vegan buttermilk.

4. Beat with a mixer until almost completely combined. Batter will be thick. Add strawberry puree and beat again. Pour half the batter into 1 cake pan.

5. Bake for 30-35 minutes or until a toothpick inserted in the center of the cake comes out clean. Remove from oven and let cool before frosting.

6. Use a vegan frosting of choice or make a butter-less buttercream with 6 tablespoons unsweetened canned coconut cream (refrigerate the can overnight) 2 tablespoons refined coconut oil, 1 and 1/4 cup powdered sugar and 1 teaspoon vanilla extract.

7. Frost and garnish with fresh blueberries and strawberries.

# EDIBLE CHOCOLATE CHIP COOKIE DOUGH

## INGREDIENTS

- 1/2 cup oat flour
- 1/4 cup melted vegan butter flavor coconut oil
- 1 tsp vanilla extract
- handful of vegan chocolate chips
- pinch of salt
- coconut sugar to taste (some like it sweeter than others)

## DIRECTIONS

1. Combine all ingredients into a mixing bowl and mix until dough is smooth and even.
2. Enjoy the cookie dough right away or try it chilled.

**PREP TIME: 5 MINUTES**
**COOK TIME: 0 MINUTES**
**TOTAL TIME: 5 MINUTES**

# CLASSIC BANANA BREAD

## INGREDIENTS

- 2 spotty bananas
- 2 eggs (or 2 flax eggs or a 1:1 vegan egg replacer)
- 1/4 cup ground flax
- 1 tsp baking powder
- 1 tbsp apple cider vinegar
- 1/3 cup avocado oil
- 1/4 cup maple syrup
- 2 cups oat flour
- 1/3 cup rolled oats
- 1 cup plant milk
- 1/2 tsp pink salt

## DIRECTIONS

1. Preheat oven to 350 F. Grease inside of a loaf pan with avocado oil.
2. In a large bowl, mash bananas. Beat eggs (or mix flax egg) and add to bowl.
3. Stir in maple syrup and oil, mixing well. Whisk together dry ingredients and add to banana mixture. Mix well and pour into prepared pan.
4. Bake 50-60 minutes or until toothpick inserted in center comes out clean. Enjoy!

**PREP TIME: 10 MINUTES**
**COOK TIME: 45-50 MINUTES**
**TOTAL TIME: 50-60 MINUTES**

# FUDGY SWEET POTATO BROWNIES

## INGREDIENTS

- 1 cup sweet potato mash
- 1 cup GF all purpose flour
- 1/2 cup almond butter
- 1/4 cup maple syrup
- 1/4 cup vegan chocolate chips
- 1/4 cup melted vegan butter flavor coconut oil or avocado oil
- 1/4 cup cocoa powder
- 2 tbsp cacao powder
- pinch of sea salt
- 1 tsp vanilla extract

## DIRECTIONS

1. Boil sweet potato and mash evenly until smooth. Preheat oven to 350 F.
2. Combine sweet potato mash and ingredients into a large mixing bowl. Mix evenly.
3. Scoop brownie batter into a greased 8x8 pan.
4. Bake for 45 minutes or until toothpick comes out clean.

**PREP TIME: 15 MINUTES**
**COOK TIME: 45 MINUTES**
**TOTAL TIME: 1 HOUR**

# ONE-BOWL ZUCCHINI BREAD

## INGREDIENTS

- 1 heaping cup grated zucchini (from one medium zucchini)
- 1 and 1/2 cup GF all purpose flour
- 1 tsp baking soda
- 1/4 teaspoon baking powder
- 2 tbsp ground flax
- 1 and 1/2 teaspoon ground cinnamon
- 1/2 tsp ginger (fresh grated works best)
- 1/2 teaspoon nutmeg
- 1/4 teaspoon cardamom
- 1 cup coconut sugar
- 1/2 cup avocado oil
- 1/2 cup oat milk or pea milk (pea milk works best)
- 1 tbsp apple cider vinegar
- 1/2 teaspoon bourbon vanilla extract
- optional: vegan chocolate chips or walnuts

**PREP TIME: 20 MINUTES**
**COOK TIME: 60 MINUTES**
**TOTAL TIME: 1 HOUR 2 MINUTES**

## DIRECTIONS

1. Preheat oven to 350 degrees F. In a small bowl, mix together dry ingredients.

2. In a separate bowl, mix together wet ingredients. Pour the wet ingredients into the dry ingredients, mixing evenly. Fold in the grated zucchini.

3. Lightly grease an 8x4 bread loaf pan. Scoop the zucchini mixture into the bread pan, smoothing the top as needed.

4. Bake zucchini bread for 50-60 minutes, until a toothpick inserted in the middle comes out clean. The top crust should be lightly browned.

4. Remove the zucchini bread from the oven. Let cool for at least 10 minutes. Slices best when fully cooled, otherwise it can be quite dense and sticky if not. Enjoy!

# VEGAN COCONUT DATE ICE CREAM

## INGREDIENTS

- 2 yellow bananas (do not use spotty ones, it doesn't taste the same!)
- 6 dates
- 1 can of full fat coconut cream
- 1 tsp vanilla extract
- 1/4 cup vegan chocolate chips
- pinch of salt

## DIRECTIONS

1. Combine all ingredients except chocolate chips in a food processor or blender and blend until creamy.
2. Pour mixture into a freezer safe storage container and freeze until solid.
3. Let that for 15 minutes or so before scooping and serving. Enjoy!

**PREP TIME: 5 MINUTES**
**COOK TIME: 0 MINUTES**
**TOTAL TIME: 5 MINUTES**

# HEALTHY HIPPIE NO BAKE COOKIES

## INGREDIENTS

- 6 dates
- 3 tbsp vegan chocolate chips
- 2 tbsp pumpkin seeds
- 1 tsp vanilla extract
- pinch of sea salt
- 2 tbsp shredded coconut
- handful of rolled oats
- 1 tbsp avocado oil
- plant milk to thin mixture

## DIRECTIONS

1. Combine all ingredients in a food processor or blender and pulse until slightly blended.
2. Scoop dough into a bowl, form dough into cookies and place onto a freezer safe baking sheet.
3. Freeze until the cookies harden or enjoy dough plain!

**PREP TIME: 5 MINUTES**
**COOK TIME: 0 MINUTES**
**TOTAL TIME: 5 MINUTES**

# VANILLA ALMOND BLUEBERRY SWEET BREAD

## INGREDIENTS

- 1/2 container unsweetened vanilla coconut milk yogurt
- 1/2 cup apple sauce
- 1 tsp cinnamon
- 1 tsp bourbon vanilla extract
- 1/3 cup ground flax
- 2 cups oat flour
- 1 cup all purpose flour
- 1 cup fresh blueberries
- 2 tbsp avocado oil
- 1 cup coconut sugar
- 1 tsp almond extract
- 1 tsp baking powder
- 1 tsp baking soda
- 2 eggs (or flax eggs, or 1:1 egg replacer)
- optional: rolled oats or slivered almonds sprinkled on top

**PREP TIME: 15 MINUTES**
**COOK TIME: 40 MINUTES**
**TOTAL TIME: 55 MINUTES**

## DIRECTIONS

1. Preheat oven to 350 F. Grease inside of a loaf pan with avocado oil.
2. In a large bowl, beat eggs (or mix flax egg) and add to bowl.
3. Stir in yogurt, apple sauce, sugar, spices and oil, mixing well. Mix together dry ingredients and add to bread mixture. Fold in blueberries, gently. Mix well and pour into prepared pan.
4. Bake 45-50 minutes or until toothpick inserted in center comes out clean. Enjoy!

# VEGAN SUPERFOOD BROWNIE BATTER

## INGREDIENTS

- 2 tbsp melted vegan butter flavor coconut oil
- 1 and 1/2 cup oat flour
- handful of vegan chocolate chips
- 1 tbsp cacao powder
- 1 tsp cocoa powder
- 2 tbsp chia seeds
- 2 tbsp flax seeds
- 1 tbsp maca powder
- 2 tbsp manuka honey or maple syrup
- 1 tbsp walnuts (optional)

## DIRECTIONS

1. Combine all ingredients into a mixing bowl and mix until dough is smooth and even.
2. Enjoy the superfood batter right away or try it chilled.

**PREP TIME: 5 MINUTES**
**COOK TIME: 0 MINUTES**
**TOTAL TIME: 5 MINUTES**

# APPLE SPIC
# OATMEA
# RAISIN
# COOKIES

## INGREDIENTS

- 1 cup rolled oats
- 1 cup apple sauce
- 1/2 cup raisins
- 2 tbsp hemp seeds
- 2 tbsp ground flax
- 1/2 tsp baking powder
- 2 heaping tbsp vegan butter flavor

  coconut oil
- pinch of salt
- 1/4 cup maple syrup
- 1 tsp vanilla extract
- 1/2 tsp cinnamon

## DIRECTIONS

1. Preheat oven to 325 F. Combine ingredients in a large mixing bowl. Mix evenly.
2. Scoop dough onto baking sheet and bake for 12 minutes or until golden brown.
3. Let cookies cool and serve. Enjoy!

**PREP TIME: 5 MINUTES**
**COOK TIME: 12 MINUTES**
**TOTAL TIME: 17 MINUTES**

# CARAMEL & CREAM CHOCOLATE DATE CANDIES

## INGREDIENTS

- 12 pitted medjool dates
- 1 tbsp lemon juice
- pinch of sea salt
- vanilla extract
- 1/2 cup vegan chocolate chips
- 1 cup vegan coconut whip (1/4 cup maple syrup, 1 can full fat coconut milk, 1 tbsp vanilla extract)
- 2 tbsp chopped walnuts

## DIRECTIONS

1. In a silicone ice cube tray, pour a layer of melted vegan chocolate chips and freeze. Since there are a few layers, this does take a little extra time to make.
2. To make homemade date caramel, place 12 dates in a food processor with 1 tbsp of lemon juice, sea salt and vanilla extract. Scoop out caramel mixture and place into silicone tray on top of first chocolate layer. Add chopped walnuts on top of date caramel
3. Next, blend together ingredients for coconut whip with a hand mixer until fluffy. Spoon this on top of the date caramel walnuts. Freeze until coconut whip is solid, then topped with a layer of melted chocolate on top. Let freeze again for about 4-5 hours. Pop the candies out like ice cubes and enjoy! Enjoy before they melt at room temperature.

**PREP TIME: 4 HOURS**
**COOK TIME: 0 MINUTES**
**TOTAL TIME: 4 HOURS**

# CLASSIC VEGAN PUMPKIN BREAD

## INGREDIENTS

- 3/4 can pumpkin puree
- 1/2 cup rolled oats
- 2 cups GF all purpose flour
- 1/2 cup maple syrup
- 1 tsp vanilla extract
- 1/4 cup ground flax
- 1 cup plant milk of choice
- 1/2 mashed banana
- 1 tsp baking powder
- 2 vegan eggs (2 flax eggs or 2 1:1 vegan egg replacers or you can use 2 real eggs if not vegan)
- pinch of salt
- 1 tsp lemon juice
- 1 tsp cinnamon
- 2 tsp pumpkin spice seasoning
- optional: 1/2 cup vegan chocolate chips

**PREP TIME: 15 MINUTES**
**COOK TIME: 45 MINUTES**
**TOTAL TIME: 1 HOUR**

## DIRECTIONS

1. Preheat oven to 350 F. Grease inside of a loaf pan with avocado oil.
2. In a large bowl, mash banana. Beat eggs (or mix flax egg) and add to bowl).
3. Stir in maple syrup, pumpkin puree and oil, mixing well. Whisk together dry ingredients. Mix well and pour into prepared pan.
4. Bake for 45 minutes or until toothpick inserted in center comes out clean. Enjoy!

# NO BAKE COCONUT DREAM BARS

## INGREDIENTS

- 3 cups shredded coconut
- 1/2 can full fat coconut cream
- 1 tbsp vanilla extract
- 1/3 cup maple syrup
- 1 tbsp water
- pinch of salt
- 1 cup vegan dark chocolate chips
- 4 tbsp coconut oil
- 2 tbsp plant milk to thin

## DIRECTIONS

1. Line 8x8 inch baking pan with parchment paper, so that the paper overhangs two sides like handles.
2. Add shredded coconut. coconut cream, vanilla, maple syrup, water and salt to a food processor or blender and blend until creamy and smooth.
3. Pour coconut mixture into baking pan.
4. Add dark chocolate chips and coconut oil to a pot and lightly cook down the chocolate chips to make a glaze. Stir well with a spatula, until smooth and combined.
5. Pour chocolate glaze over the coconut mixture. Garnish with shredded coconut.
6. Refrigerate for at least 1.5 hours before serving. Cut into bars, store in a container in the fridge at all times as it will melt at room temperature.

**PREP TIME: 10 MINUTES**
**COOK TIME: 0 MINUTES**
**TOTAL TIME: 10 MINUTES**

# GROCERY

# STAPLES

Starting with family members and friends, then to our Instagram followers...behold...the infamous "grocery list." We are not doctors or Registered Dietitians, so please ask yours before you make any dietary changes. This is simply a lifestyle and is what works for our families! With that said, here are the staples we use in our homes. We practice shopping the outside aisles first, which is where the fresh food and produce are, and where we shop the bulk of the groceries. The center aisles are usually the more processed goods, so we try to stick the outside aisles to keep things even healthier and fresher.

PS: This isn't what we buy every week because 1. that would be insane and 2. expensive. These are simply staples we like to have on hand. Enjoy!

# produce

- Bananas
- Apples
- Pears
- Berries or in season fruit (peaches, plums, etc)
- Sweet potatoes
- Yellow or red Potatoes
- Melon
- Grapes
- Avocado
- Lettuce
- Spinach
- Kale
- Onion
- Mushroom
- Baby tomatoes
- Yellow, red & green bell peppers
- Cucumber
- Zucchini
- Carrots

Fresh items
- Fresh salsa (can only be found in produce aisle because it's fresh!) or natural/homemade salsa
- Organic hummus
- Coconut yogurt (is found near dairy/produce)
- Frozen fruit

# dry goods

- Gluten-free rolled oats
- Gluten-free oat flour
- Gluten-free brown rice pasta
- Lentil pasta
- Chickpea pasta
- Organic pasta sauce
- Quinoa
- Brown rice
- Basmati rice
- Raisins
- Rice cakes
- Cacao powder
- Hemp seeds
- Maca powder
- Coconut shreds
- Hemp powder
- Dates
- Vegan egg replacer

Nuts & seeds
- Almonds
- Walnuts
- Cashews
- Pumpkin seeds
- Ground flax seeds
- Chia seeds

# condiments

- Organic ketchup
- Organic spicy mustard
- Organic yellow mustard
- Coconut aminos
- Vegan mayo
- Kalamata olives
- Vegan butter
- Vegan cheese
- Honey
- Maple syrup
- Coconut sugar
- Coconut cream

Oils & vinegars
- Avocado oil
- Extra virgin olive oil
- Coconut oil
- Balsamic vinegar
- Apple cider vinegar
- Hot sauce

Nut & seed butters
- Sun butter
- Almond butter
- Coconut butter
- Cashew butter

# herbs & spices

- Pink himalayan sea salt
- Cinnamon
- Curry powder
- Garlic Powder
- Fresh garlic
- Nutritional yeast
- Cracked black pepper
- Cayenne
- Basil
- Oregano
- Onion Powder
- Chili powder
- Paprika
- Pumpkin pie spice
- Cardamom
- Allspice
- Thyme
- Sage
- Cumin
- Ginger
- Nutmeg
- Dill

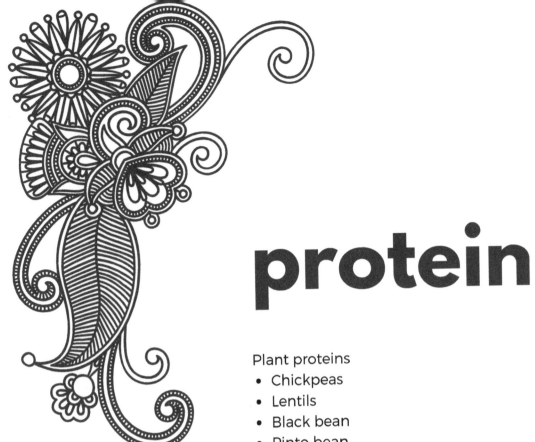

# protein

Plant proteins
- Chickpeas
- Lentils
- Black bean
- Pinto bean
- White bean
- Kidney bean
- Quinoa
- Hemp seeds
- Vegan protein powder
- Veggie burgers

Animal proteins
- Organic cage-free eggs
- Organic chicken
- Grass fed beef (organic)
- Organic chicken sausage
- Organic ground turkey

# beverage

- Almond milk
- Flax milk
- Oat milk
- Coconut milk
- Organic coffee
- Matcha tea
- Herbal tea bags
- Kombucha
- Green juice
- Organic red wine (on occasion)

# extra

- Vegan Ice cream (everything in moderation!)
- Vegan chocolate chips
- Vegan popcorn
- Vegan chocolate bars
- Grain-free chips (made from beans, coconut or cassava)
- Grain-free wraps
- Gluten-free vegan bread
- Plantain chips
- Vegan protein bars

# HEALTHY
# SWAPS &

# NUTRITION
# TIPS

# Healthier Swaps

## IN THE KITCHEN

# BEST OIL CHOICES

- Avocado oil
- Coconut oil
- Walnut oil
- Macadamia nut oil
- Olive oil
- Algal oil
- Hemp oil
- Pumpkin seed oil

# BEST OIL-FREE SWAPS
## (1:1 REPLACEMENTS)

- Apple sauce
- Banana
- Pumpkin
- Avocado
- Vegan greek yogurt
- Coconut cream
- Squash
- Sweet potato puree

# BEST EGG-FREE SWAPS
# (RATIOS FOR ONE EGG)

- Apple sauce (1/4 cup)
- Banana  (1/2 banana)
- Pumpkin (1/4 cup)
- Avocado (1/4 cup)
- Vegan greek yogurt (1/4 cup)
- Coconut cream (1/4 cup)
- Squash (1/4 cup)
- Flax (flax egg = 1 tbsp ground flax + 3 tbsp water)
- Chia (chia egg = 1 tbsp chia seeds + 1/3 cup water
- Nut butters (3 tbsp)
- Agar agar (1 tbsp + 1 tbsp water)
- Sweet potato puree (1/4 cup)

# BEST GF FLOUR CHOICES

- Oat flour
- Almond flour
- Coconut flour
- Rice flour
- Buckwheat flour
- Chickpea flour
- Cassava flour
- Quinoa flour
- Arrowroot
- Sorghum flour
- Amaranth flour

# BEST DAIRY-FREE MILK CHOICES

- Almond milk
- Coconut milk
- Oat milk
- Hemp milk
- Pea milk
- Hazelnut milk
- Walnut milk
- Macadamia milk
- Flax milk
- Rice milk
- Cashew milk

## BEST DAIRY-FREE
## CHEESE CHOICES

- Almond based cheese
- Coconut based cheese
- Cashew based cheese
- Nutritional yeast
- Vegan parmesean
- Vegan cheese singles
- Vegan cheese shreds

# BETTER SWEETENER CHOICES

- Coconut sugar
- Maple syrup
- Dates
- Date sugar
- Honey
- Stevia
- Monk fruit
- Brown rice syrup

# DIRTY DOZEN (FOODS TO BUY ORGANIC)

- Strawberries
- Spinach
- Kale
- Nectarines
- Apples
- Grapes
- Peaches
- Cherries
- Pears
- Tomatoes
- Celery
- Potatoes

# CLEAN FIFTEEN (FOODS THAT ARE OKAY NON-ORGANIC)

- Sweet peas
- Onions
- Avocados
- Asparagus
- Mangoes
- Pineapples
- Cabbage
- Eggplant
- Honeydew
- Papayas
- Kiwi
- Cantaloupe
- Broccoli
- Cauliflower
- Honeydew

# WHY EAT PLANT HEAVY?

*Plant-heavy diets are naturally low in saturated fat, free of cholesterol. They are also high in fiber, vitamins, minerals and antioxidants. Not only does the extra fiber from fruits, vegetables, grains and legumes help improve digestion, these plant-based foods are more nutrient-dense than processed foods. A plant-heavy diet has many healthy benefits, including lowering your risk of heart disease, certain cancers, obesity, diabetes, and may also improve mental and brain health. As a bonus, a plant-heavy diet is an environmentally friendly choice for the planet and promotes the well-being of animals.*

# WHY NO REFINED SUGAR?

*Our recipes do not contain refined sugar. Since the body breaks down refined sugar so rapidly, it causes our insulin and blood sugar levels to spike. When that happens, you don't feel full after you're done eating, no matter how many calories you consumed. It is also more heavily processed and lacks nutrition in comparison to the natural plant-based sweeteners we use.*

# WHY COOKING OIL MATTERS?

*Cooking oil can get confusing, so we want to simplify the reasons we use the oils we use. When it comes to oil, not all are created equally. Some oils promote health while others may destroy it. While vegetable oil may sound healthy, it's one of the worst oils we can consume, right alongside canola oil. These two oils are often highly processed, high in inflammatory omega-6 fatty acids while also lacking heart-healthy omega-3 fatty acids. The excessive processing of these harmful oils may also promote disease. The oils we use are unrefined, have many health benefits and contain essential nutrients.*

# WHY ORGANIC MATTERS?

*It is not always necessary or affordable to purchase organic foods, but sometimes it can be worth it. Recent studies have shown that organic foods are not only clear of harmful pesticides, fungicides, heavy metals, antibiotics or toxic compounds, but they may also be richer in antioxidants. By eating organic, we simply eliminate the yucky stuff and maximize the nutrient value of our food.*

# WHY INGREDIENTS MATTER?

*Simple is better. And the same is true for the ingredients in our food. If you can't pronounce the ingredients in your food, or there are way too many ingredients involved, chances are it's not natural enough to be consuming on a regular basis.*
*Simple foods typically mean less processed and more natural. When choosing ingredients, shoot for the ones with lower processing (unrefined), and steer clear from white sugar, white flours, dairy products, chemicals, artificial colors or flavors, MSG, nitrates, preservatives, artificial sweeteners and hydrogenated oils.*

*"Cooking healthy meals for my family is empowering.
I feel great honor in filling the bellies of my loved ones with delicious,
whole plant-based foods. It will always be special and sacred to me."
- Brittany Bacinski*

# BUFF BABES TO BALANCED MAMAS

*Everyone has a story and it all starts somewhere. This is ours. From "buff bodybuilding babes" with similar pasts of diet extremes, to finally achieving a balanced lifestyle in nutrition, health and total wellness. We believe the food we eat is more than just a meal, it's a conscious choice to nourish the body from the inside out. Because to us, health really is wealth. Eat like a hippie!*

# *Amber Fokken*

FITNESS MODEL, INFLUENCER,
ADO FITNESS OWNER & MAMA

@mishkadawn

# *Brittany Bacinski*

WELLNESS BLOGGER, WRITER,
AUTHOR & MAMA

@brittanybacinski

*Thank you so much for trusting us with putting a few new meals on your table. We hope they become instant classics and family favorites for years to come.*

**Peace, love & plants,**
**Amber & Brittany**

CPSIA information can be obtained
at www.ICGtesting.com
Printed in the USA
LVHW072351090420
652894LV00017B/829